STEM

Mission to Mars

Problem Solving

Rane Anderson

Consultants

Michele Ogden, Ed.D
Principal, Irvine Unified School District

Jennifer Robertson, M.A.Ed.
Teacher, Huntington Beach City School District

Publishing Credits
Rachelle Cracchiolo, M.S.Ed., *Publisher*
Conni Medina, M.A.Ed., *Managing Editor*
Dona Herweck Rice, *Series Developer*
Emily R. Smith, M.A.Ed., *Series Developer*
Diana Kenney, M.A.Ed., NBCT, *Content Director*
Stacy Monsman, M.A., *Editor*
Kevin Panter, *Graphic Designer*

Image Credits: pp. 4-5, 25 (bottom) NASA/JPL/Cornell; p. 5 Linda Moon/Shutterstock.com; pp. 6, 7 (top and bottom), 15, 16, 17, 20-21, 21, 27 NASA; pp. 8, 25 (top) NASA/JPL-Caltech/Univ. of Arizona; p. 9 NASA/JPL-Caltech/MSSS; pp. 10-11, 16-17 NASA/JPL; pp. 12-13 Photos courtesy of NASA/Regan Geeseman; p. 14 Dave Mosher; p. 18 NASA/JPL-Caltech/ESA/DLR/FU Berlin/MSSS; p. 19 NASA/JPL-Caltech; p. 22 NASA Photo/Alamy Stock Photo; p. 23 (top) Jim Olive/Polaris/Newscom, (bottom) Volker Steger/Science Source; pp. 24-25 NASA/JPL/Arizona State University, R. Luk; p. 26 Image Source/Getty Images; p.28 Dava Newman/NASA/AFLO/Newscom; p. 31 NASA/JSC; all other images from iStock and/or Shutterstock.

Teacher Created Materials
5301 Oceanus Drive
Huntington Beach, CA 92649-1030
http://www.tcmpub.com

ISBN 978-1-4807-5801-8

Table of Contents

Destination: Mars 4

Prepare for Takeoff...6

Rockets to Mars.. 14

On Mars 20

Signs of Life?... 24

The Mars Countdown...26

Problem Solving 28

Glossary...30

Index..31

Answer Key..32

Destination: Mars

What will it take to safely send humans to Mars? And how will they survive? Scientists have asked these questions for years. They are still trying to answer them today. After all, Mars is a dangerous and deadly place for humans.

Its thin **atmosphere** lets in too much **radiation** from the sun. That could make humans sick. And the air pressure on Mars is way too low. That means that humans not wearing space suits outside would swell up like balloons and die. And those are just two things that could go wrong. Traveling to Mars is very dangerous.

So, why go? There is so much to learn! Scientists have already started planning for the trip. The National Aeronautics and Space Administration (NASA) wants to get humans to Mars by the 2030s. Can they do it?

Mars

Astronaut Scott Kelly puts away fruit on the International Space Station.

Prepare for Takeoff

What is the best way to learn about space? By living there, of course! From March 2015 to March 2016, two **astronauts** did just that. Scott Kelly and Mikhail Kornienko lived on the **International Space Station** (ISS). They spent nearly a year tracking their health. They took blood and urine samples. They used an **ultrasound** machine to monitor their hearts and eyes.

Space is a harsh place. Astronauts are exposed to radiation. Their muscles get weaker. And their diets are limited. But, people believe time on the ISS is worth it. Data from the yearlong mission will help NASA. NASA plans to use the data collected to figure out how to take care of humans on a trip to Mars. NASA hopes to keep the Mars crew healthy in space for a long time. Since it is a long trip to Mars, this is crucial!

Mikhail Kornienko

the International Space Station

Exploring with Rovers

Humans have not yet made it to Mars. But, robots from Earth have. These missions have taught scientists a lot about the Red Planet. NASA **rovers** have been searching the surface of Mars. They are like robot scientists. Rovers gather data that helps NASA plan for future trips.

The youngest rover on Mars is Curiosity. It touched down on August 6, 2012. It has a lot of tools. The tools help it collect data about the rocks and soil. It even has an arm that can hold and move its tools. And it has a laser that can burn holes through rocks!

Curiosity can do lots of things. But it still needs someone to control it. Scientists must tell it what to do before it can perform a task.

The yellow path shows Curiosity's route on the surface of Mars.

If Curiosity can travel 200 meters per day, how many days will it take to travel 800 meters?

1. Write an equation and find the solution. Let d stand for the days traveled.

2. Imagine that one of Curiosity's wheels is broken and will not turn. It can now only travel 100 meters per day. How many days will it take for the rover to cover 800 meters? Write an equation and find the solution, using d to stand for days traveled.

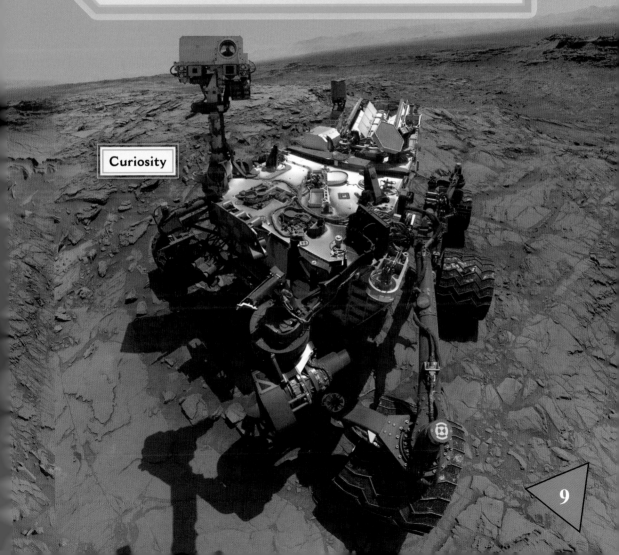

Curiosity

9

There are times when NASA loses all contact with rovers on Mars. This happens when Earth and Mars are on opposite sides of the sun. Loss of contact can last for over a month! This is one problem NASA wants to learn more about. People at NASA must learn how to stay in touch with the rovers. Once a crew gets to Mars, they want to be sure they can talk to them at all times.

As of 2016, NASA could send signals to the rover most of the time. And it sent signals back. But there was still a delay of 3 to 22 minutes. That long wait meant they would not be able to talk to a crew in real time. In an emergency, the Mars crew would be on its own for a while.

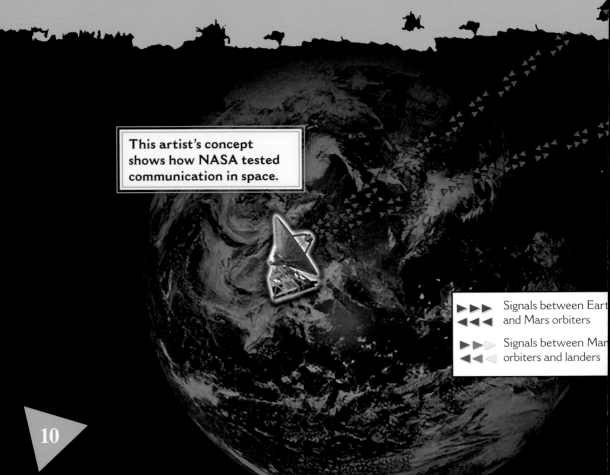

This artist's concept shows how NASA tested communication in space.

▶▶▶ Signals between Eart
◀◀◀ and Mars orbiters

▶▶▷ Signals between Mar
◀◀◁ orbiters and landers

If it takes at least 3 minutes to send a one-way signal from Earth to Mars, a round-trip signal would take 6 minutes.

1. How long would it take to send 6 round-trip signals?

2. When Mars and Earth are farthest from each other, it takes about 7 times as long to send signals. In these equations, t represents the amount of time it will take. Which equation can be used to represent the time it would take to send 2 round-trip signals?

$$2 \times 6 \times 7 = t \qquad\qquad 2 \times 6 + t = 7$$

$$2 \times 6 \times t = 7 \qquad\qquad 2 \times 6 + 7 = t$$

A geologist examines samples in the desert, using equipment that can be used in space.

Exploring Mars-like Places

There are places on Earth where it is not easy to survive. The Arctic can be just as tough to live in as scorching hot deserts. Places like these can test a person's mental and physical strength. NASA knows that these can be the best places to research.

Much of Mars's surface has huge sand dunes. The Arizona deserts have those, too. So, a group of NASA scientists moved into an **analog** there. An analog is a shelter for living and working. It has conditions similar to those of space. This helps prepare people for Mars. Scientists can also wear gear and pretend they are on Mars. They can hike up sand dunes and collect samples. They can even use the same tools they will have on Mars.

LET'S EXPLORE MATH

Imagine that the Mars crew has planted 11 pea plants in a desert greenhouse. Each plant can produce enough peas to fill 9 bowls. How many bowls of peas will the crew get in total from their harvest?

1. Estimate the number of bowls of peas the crew will be able to fill.

2. How many bowls will actually be filled? Use your estimate to check if your solution is reasonable.

Rockets to Mars

Earth and Mars move on their own paths around the sun. These paths are called *orbits*, and they are shaped like **ellipses**. Earth and Mars are not always the same distance from each other. At their closest, Mars is about 34 million miles (55 million kilometers) from Earth. That is more than 4,000 times the width of Earth! So, the best time to go to Mars is when it is as close to Earth as possible.

A trip to Mars takes about eight months. That is a long time. So, the crew has to be prepared. NASA has to make sure the crew will have enough water to drink. Water is heavy. The ship will not be able to carry all of the water that they will need. So, NASA is testing ways to have the crew make water with their urine and sweat! They should be able to filter most of these fluids into water that they can drink.

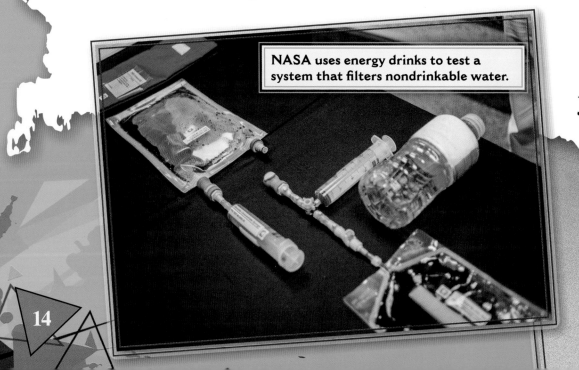

NASA uses energy drinks to test a system that filters nondrinkable water.

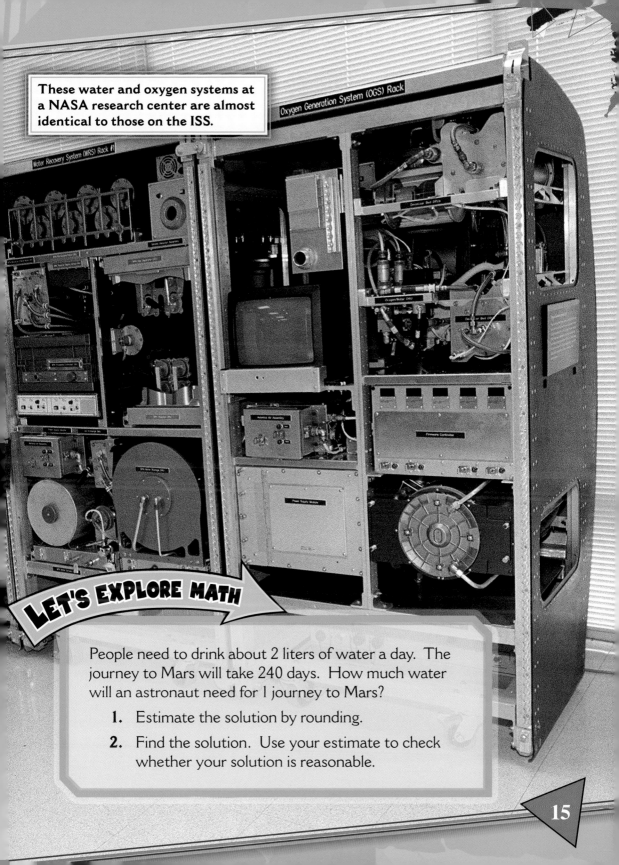

These water and oxygen systems at a NASA research center are almost identical to those on the ISS.

Oxygen Generation System (OGS) Rack

Water Recovery System (WRS) Rack

LET'S EXPLORE MATH

People need to drink about 2 liters of water a day. The journey to Mars will take 240 days. How much water will an astronaut need for 1 journey to Mars?

1. Estimate the solution by rounding.

2. Find the solution. Use your estimate to check whether your solution is reasonable.

The Mars crew will need to take a lot of **cargo** with them. They will need food, water, and tools. The Mars crew will rely completely on what they bring. After all, they won't be able to return to Earth if they forget something. But the spacecraft can't be too heavy. If it is, the rockets might not have enough power to **propel** it out to space.

So, scientists have made a plan. They will sort the cargo into groups. Groups of cargo will be sent into space a few at a time. Once the cargo ships land on Mars, it will be the crew's turn to go.

A cargo ship approaches the ISS.

This artist's concept shows how NASA plans to grow fresh food on other planets.

Nobody can agree on where the crew's spacecraft should land on Mars. They want a spot that will be safe. They also want it to land where they will learn the most about Mars. But more than anything, they want it to land in the spot they choose!

In the past, rovers did not land in the right spot. At that time, scientists could only get rovers to land in a large zone. The zone could be up to 500 square mi. (1,300 square km). That is the size of Hong Kong! The Mars crew won't want to land hundreds of miles from their supplies. That would be a disaster!

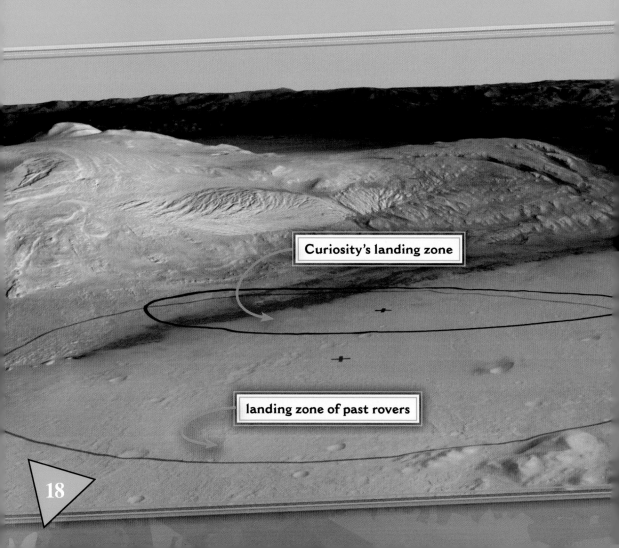

Curiosity's landing zone

landing zone of past rovers

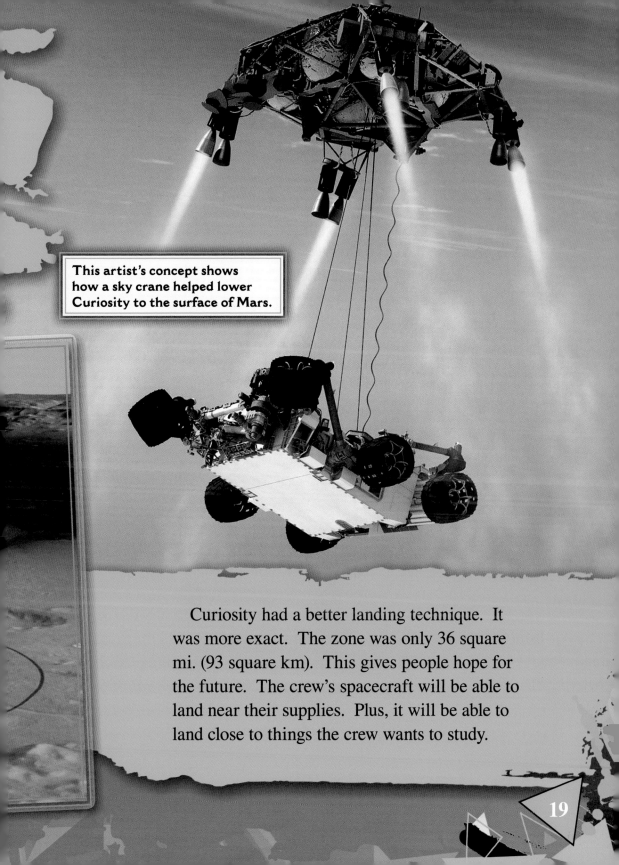

This artist's concept shows how a sky crane helped lower Curiosity to the surface of Mars.

Curiosity had a better landing technique. It was more exact. The zone was only 36 square mi. (93 square km). This gives people hope for the future. The crew's spacecraft will be able to land near their supplies. Plus, it will be able to land close to things the crew wants to study.

On Mars

Once people get to Mars, they will need a safe place to live. Scientists are trying to build such a **habitat**. They nicknamed it the Hab. The Hab will have beds and showers. There will also be a bathroom, a kitchen, and an exercise room. But even astronauts need to have some fun. In the Hab, they will be able to talk, read books, watch movies, or even play musical instruments. These are all things people have done on other space missions.

People will live and work in the Hab. So, there will be parts of it that are reserved for work. A large storage room will keep equipment safe. The Hab will also have a lab where the crew can study what they find.

Habitat Demonstration Unit

There will be ways to track conditions and communicate outside and inside the Hab. There will be a main control panel to contact the crew on Earth. And people inside the Hab will be able to speak with the team that is working outside. Another panel helps keep an eye on conditions in the Hab. Is there an oxygen leak? Is the air pressure good? The panel will alert them if problems arise.

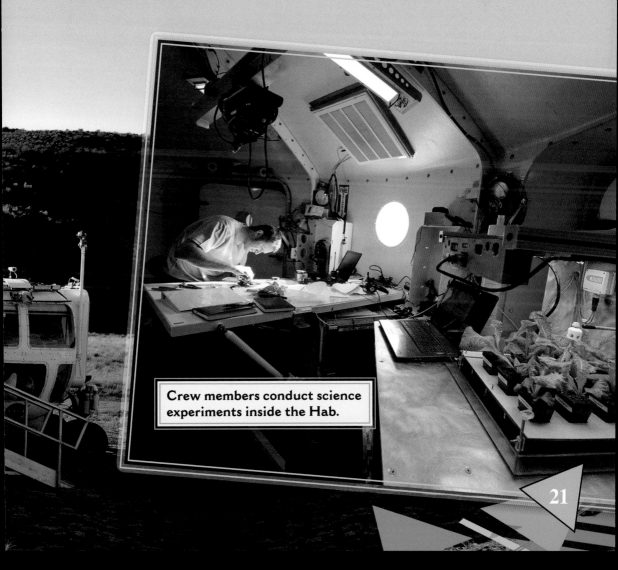

Crew members conduct science experiments inside the Hab.

A New Suit

While on Mars, the crew will need a special kind of space suit. In the past, space suits were big and bulky. But the Mars crew will need to hike, move, and work with tools for long hours. The suits will need to be strong enough for life on Mars. But they will also need to allow people to move around easily.

Professor Dava Newman thought she could help. She and her students work and study at Massachusetts Institute of Technology (MIT). They made a new suit for NASA. Their BioSuit™ will help the crew work while also keeping them safe. NASA says the suit is like a "second-skin." It is not bulky like suits of the past. Instead, it presses and molds to the body. The fabric makes it more comfortable. The crew will be able to move and work more easily.

Professor Dava Newman

Newman tests the BioSuit in a wind tunnel.

A researcher adjusts the BioSuit.

23

Signs of Life?

Scientists want to know: is there life on Mars? So far, rovers have not found any evidence of life on this dry, dusty planet. But, there are clues that water might have flowed on Mars. And wherever there is water, there could be life.

Pictures from Mars have shown huge cracks in the mud on its surface. The cracks might have formed after a lake dried up. Scientists have also found sand and dirt inside a crater. Did water carry it there? Scientists see dark streaks in pictures taken during warmer seasons. Those same streaks fade in pictures taken during colder seasons. Scientists believe those streaks could be water that is melting and freezing.

The future Mars crew will investigate these clues. They will continue to look for water. If they find it, they might also find signs of life.

Dark streaks at the bottom of the Hale Crater could be signs of water (color added to pictures for identification purposes).

The sphere-like "rocks" in this Mars image could have formed with wet sediment (colored blue for easy identification).

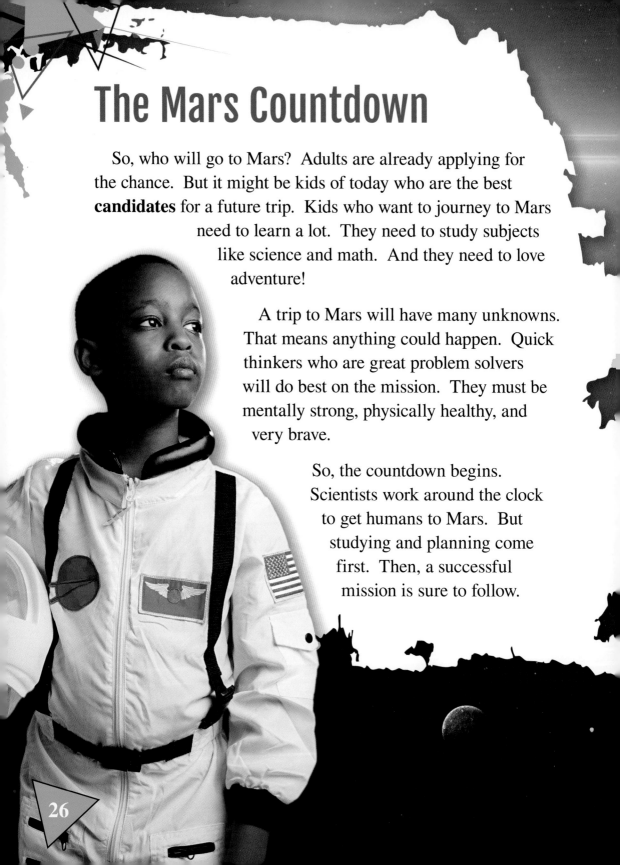

The Mars Countdown

So, who will go to Mars? Adults are already applying for the chance. But it might be kids of today who are the best **candidates** for a future trip. Kids who want to journey to Mars need to learn a lot. They need to study subjects like science and math. And they need to love adventure!

A trip to Mars will have many unknowns. That means anything could happen. Quick thinkers who are great problem solvers will do best on the mission. They must be mentally strong, physically healthy, and very brave.

So, the countdown begins. Scientists work around the clock to get humans to Mars. But studying and planning come first. Then, a successful mission is sure to follow.

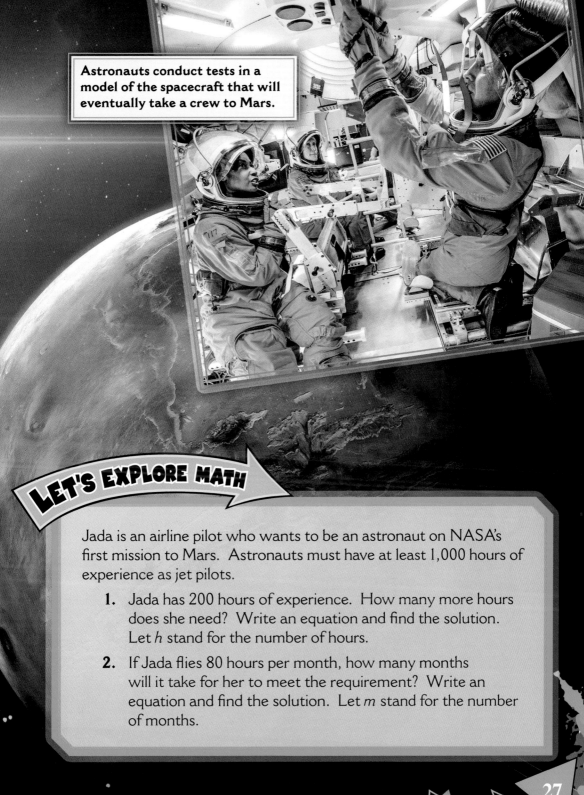

Astronauts conduct tests in a model of the spacecraft that will eventually take a crew to Mars.

LET'S EXPLORE MATH

Jada is an airline pilot who wants to be an astronaut on NASA's first mission to Mars. Astronauts must have at least 1,000 hours of experience as jet pilots.

1. Jada has 200 hours of experience. How many more hours does she need? Write an equation and find the solution. Let h stand for the number of hours.

2. If Jada flies 80 hours per month, how many months will it take for her to meet the requirement? Write an equation and find the solution. Let m stand for the number of months.

⚙ Problem Solving

After many months of traveling through space, the Mars crew will touch down on the Red Planet. They will set up the Hab. They will get their supplies and equipment in order. But then, it will be time to get to work! The crew will need to conduct research. They will have to work outside much of the time. As long as they are in their space suits, it will be safe to be outside. Their space suits will help them breathe. The suits will hold enough oxygen for crew members to work outside for up to 8 hours at a time.

1. How many minutes will crew members be able to work outside before their oxygen runs out?

2. If a crew member needs to collect 40 samples, how many minutes can be spent collecting each sample before running out of oxygen? Write an equation and find the solution. Use m to stand for the number of minutes a crew member could spend collecting each sample.

3. Imagine that crew members figure out a way to upgrade their space suits. Now, they can work outside for 9 hours at a time. Assume they spend the same number of minutes collecting each sample. How many more samples could be collected in that extra hour? Write an equation and find the solution. Use s to represent the number of samples.

4. Two crew members collected 80 samples total. They divide the samples equally to carry them back to the Hab. On the way back, each of them picks up 5 new samples. How many samples will each crew member deliver?

Glossary

analog—situation on Earth that mimics the physical and mental effects of space on humans

astronauts—people who travel to space

atmosphere—the gases that surround a planet or star

candidates—people who are being considered for a job, position, or award

cargo—goods that are carried from one place to another on a ship, aircraft, or motor vehicle

ellipses—shapes that look like flattened circles

habitat—the type of place where a plant or animal naturally lives or grows

International Space Station—a human-made satellite orbiting Earth where astronauts conduct space research

propel—to drive something forward

radiation—a type of powerful energy that is produced by nuclear reactions

rovers—vehicles used for exploring the surfaces of planets or moons

ultrasound—a method of producing images of the inside of the body by using a machine that produces sound waves

Index

air pressure, 4, 21

Arctic, 13

atmosphere, 4

BioSuit, 22–23

Curiosity, 8–9, 18–19

greenhouse, 13

Hab, 20–21, 28–29

International Space Station
    (ISS), 6–7

Kelly, Scott, 6

Kornienko, Mikhail, 6–7

National Aeronautics and
    Space Administration
    (NASA), 4, 6, 8, 10, 13–14,
    16, 22, 27

Newman, Dava, 22–23

radiation, 4, 6

rovers, 8–10, 18, 24

space, 6, 10, 12–13, 17, 20, 28

space suits, 4, 22, 28–29

Answer Key

Let's Explore Math

page 9:

1. $200 \times d = 800$; $d = 4$ days
2. $100 \times d = 800$; $d = 8$ days

page 11:

1. 36 minutes
2. $2 \times 6 \times 7 = t$

page 13:

1. Answers will vary but may include 10 pea plants × 10 bowls per plant = 100 bowls total.
2. 99 bowls total; the estimate is reasonable

page 15:

1. Answers will vary but may include $2 \times 200 = 400$ liters
2. $2 \times 240 = 480$ liters a day; the estimate is reasonable

page 27:

1. $200 + h = 1,000$ or $1,000 - 200 = h$; $h = 800$ hours
2. $80 \times m = 800$ or $800 \div 80 = m$; $m = 10$ months

Problem Solving

1. 480 minutes
2. $40 \times m = 480$ or $480 \div 40 = m$; $m = 12$ minutes per sample
3. $12 \times s = 60$ or $60 \div 12 = s$; $s = 5$ extra samples
4. 45 samples each